anythink

1859

The first anaerobic digestion plant is built in Bombay, India, to provide energy for a leper colony.

2011

F[...] supports the development of safer, more efficient toilets in the developing world with the "Reinvent the Toilet Challenge."

1640s

Jan Baptist van Helmont works out that flammable gases can arise from feces.

1829

English scholar William Buckland publishes the first ever paper on coprolites (fossil feces).

1860s

European settlers of the Great Plains, lacking wood and coal, use buffalo manure to provide fuel for heat and cooking.

2014

The world's first "poo bus," fueled by human waste, goes into service in Bristol, England.

The Poop Cycle

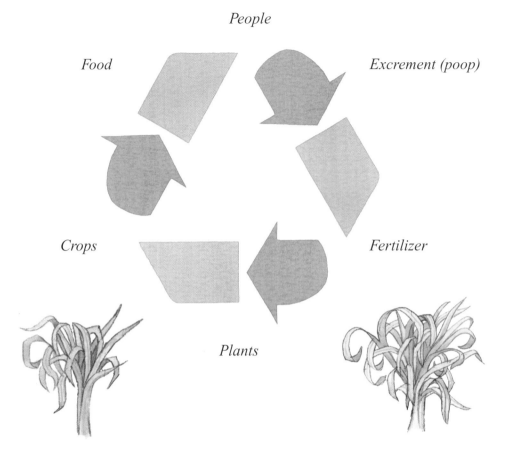

People

Food

Excrement (poop)

Crops

Fertilizer

Plants

When you go to the bathroom, it may seem like the end of a process, but it's not. Your poop gets taken to a sewage treatment plant where it is filtered and cleaned. The nutrient-rich sludge that remains, known as "biosolids," is sold to farmers as fertilizer. The fertilizer helps the farmers grow crops. Those crops are eaten as food by you and animals. Those animals may also become food that you eat. After you've digested the food, you excrete it. So going to the bathroom is not the end of the process, but one stage in a cycle—the poop cycle.

Author:

Alex Woolf studied history at Essex University, England. He is the author of over 60 books for children, many of them on historical topics. They include *You Wouldn't Want to Live Without Books!,* *You Wouldn't Want to Live Without Money!,* and *You Wouldn't Want to Live Without Vegetables!*

Artist:

David Antram was born in Brighton, England, in 1958. He studied at Eastbourne College of Art and then worked in advertising for 15 years before becoming a full-time artist. He has illustrated many children's nonfiction books.

Series creator:

David Salariya was born in Dundee, Scotland. He has illustrated a wide range of books and has created and designed many new series for publishers in the UK and overseas. David established The Salariya Book Company in 1989. He lives in Brighton with his wife, illustrator Shirley Willis, and their son, Jonathan.

Editor: **Jacqueline Ford**

Editorial Assistant: **Mark Williams**

PAPER FROM
SUSTAINABLE
FORESTS

© The Salariya Book Company Ltd MMXVI

Published in Great Britain in 2016 by
The Salariya Book Company Ltd
25 Marlborough Place, Brighton BN1 1UB

ISBN-13: 978-0-531-21489-3 (lib. bdg.) 978-0-531-22439-7 (pbk.)

Published in 2016 in the United States
by Franklin Watts
An imprint of Scholastic Inc.

A CIP catalog record for this book is available
from the Library of Congress.

Printed and bound in China.
Printed on paper from sustainable sources.
1 2 3 4 5 6 7 8 9 10 R 25 24 23 22 21 20 19 18 17 16

You Wouldn't Want to Live Without™

Poop!

Written by
Alex Woolf

Illustrated by
David Antram

Series created by
David Salariya

Franklin Watts®
An Imprint of Scholastic Inc.

Contents

Introduction

What if we didn't have poop? What would happen to the parts of food our bodies don't need? And how would we produce healthy crops? Usually we don't like to talk about it, but going to the bathroom is a natural and necessary part of our lives. We eat, we digest our food, and what our body can't digest, it gets rid of in the form of poop. There are some parts of food that contain no nutrients. In other words, they contain nothing that our bodies can use for energy, growth, or health—and those parts must be ejected. If they weren't, they would remain in our bodies and make us sick. But poop is useful not just as a way of getting rid of waste. It can also be used to power our cars, heat our homes, and help grow our crops, as well as lots of other useful things. Read on to learn why you wouldn't want to live without poop.

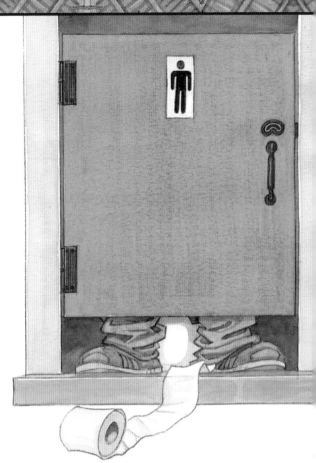

What Is Poop?

Digestion*

1. Stomach: Juices break food down and release the nutrients. The broken-down food is then pumped into the small intestine.

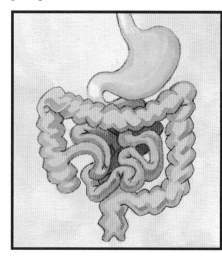

Poop is the solid or semisolid stuff that we pass out of our bodies when we go to the bathroom. About 75 percent of it is made up of water. The rest of it is made up of dead bacteria (germs) that help us digest our food, living bacteria, undigested bits of food (fiber), and various substances from our bodies such as mucus. Poop is usually brown, but it can sometimes be green, for example, if we eat a lot of green, leafy vegetables. It smells bad because the bacteria in the poop produces smelly gases.

Each organ discussed is shown in green.

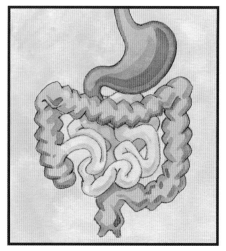

2. Small intestine: Fluids from the liver and pancreas help turn nutrients into useful substances such as glucose, which then pass into the bloodstream.

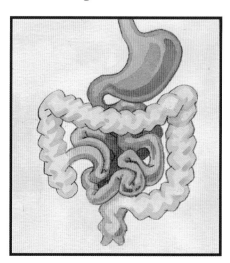

3. Large intestine: The leftover material continues to the large intestine, or colon, which turns it into poop. The poop passes out of your colon through the anus.

Please, sir!

NEEDING TO GO. Poop gets stored in the colon. When the colon is full, a signal is sent to your brain and you get the urge to go to the bathroom.

Whole-wheat flour, nuts, and vegetables all contain fiber, which helps keep your bowel movements regular.

Should be finished in an hour.

WHEN YOU CAN'T GO.
If the poop is stored in the colon for too long, it becomes dry and hard to pass. This is called constipation. One common cause of constipation is not having enough fiber in your diet. Fiber helps waste move along through your intestines.

DREADFUL DIARRHEA.
When you have to go to the bathroom frequently and you produce loose, watery poop, you have diarrhea. This is often caused by food poisoning or a stomach virus.

7

What Are the Dangers of Poop?

Poop contains bacteria, which are tiny organisms, and some of these can harm our health. In the developed world, the vast majority of people have flushing toilets connected to sewage systems that wash our feces safely away. But people in developing countries do not always have access to this kind of sanitation. Sometimes they must defecate in the open, and bacteria from their feces can contaminate local water supplies or be spread to the community by houseflies. This can cause deadly diseases such as typhoid fever and cholera. But it's not just people in developing countries who are in danger. People everywhere risk catching or spreading disease if they don't wash their hands properly after going to the bathroom.

BACTERIA are tiny one-celled organisms that can live in our bodies. Some kinds of bacteria help us with digestion. Others, like Salmonella, are germs that can cause disease.

Where are all the fish?

DIRTY WATER. About 40 percent of the world's population lives in places where human and animal waste flows untreated, straight into rivers, the ocean, or underground water sources.

DOG POOP can be dangerous, as it may contain the parasite *Toxocara canis* (roundworm), which can cause blindness in humans. That's why it's important to dispose of dog waste correctly.

CAT PARASITES. Some cat poop contains parasites that can infect pregnant women, causing possible problems in the baby. Always dispose of cat litter in the trash can, not down the toilet.

FOUL FOWL. Birds like pigeons, geese, starlings, and sparrows can carry up to 60 disease-producing bacteria in their droppings, including some that cause respiratory and skin diseases.

What About Animal Poop?

Of course it's not just humans that poop. Animals do it as well. Some of the bigger animals poop a lot: The average elephant produces around 110 pounds (50 kilograms) of dung a day! Some animals *eat* poop! The dung beetle and the housefly consume the feces of larger animals—if it weren't for them, the world would be overrun with poop! But we shouldn't only think of poop as something disgusting. It also has its uses. For example, the trees of the Amazon rain forest rely on tambaqui fish to spread their seeds by eating them and then excreting them somewhere else.

PROJECTILE Poop. When the Adélie penguin needs to go, it perches on the edge of its nest, rear end facing outward, and shoots out its poop up to 4.5 feet (1.4 meters) into the distance.

POOP-EATERS. The capybara of South America eats grass, bark, plants, and fruit. The soft, green poop it produces still contains some nutrition, so it eats that as well!

THE POOP DANCE. Some sloths climb down from trees only once a week so they can poop. They do a strange hip-swaying dance at the base of the tree as they do their business.

DISGUISED AS DROPPINGS. The bird-dropping spider of Australia is so named because it disguises itself as bird dung to avoid being eaten by birds.

How It Works

Why do dogs sometimes spin around before they poop? Dogs can sense Earth's magnetic field and like to position themselves in a north-south direction. Why? Nobody knows!

Lunch has been served!

How Do Animals Make Use of Poop?

A nimals have found all sorts of weird and wonderful uses for their waste. For example, the larvae of some leaf beetles build mobile homes out of their own poop. Big cats, monkeys, and wolves use their urine or feces to mark out their territory and warn other animals to keep away. Some animals make use of other animals' poop. For instance, a South American parasite hides in bird poop waiting for an ant to eat it. The parasite then makes the ant's abdomen swell up like a berry. A bird, thinking it's found a berry, eats it. The parasite's eggs end up in the bird's poop, and the cycle starts all over again.

Now don't fall off!

CUBIC POOP. Wombats excrete dice-shaped poop. Why? Because they use it to mark their territory and ward off other wombats, and round poops would simply roll away.

TERMITE FARMERS. Some termites grow fungus gardens out of a bed of their own poop. They grow them inside large, temperature-controlled mounds built out of soil, saliva, and feces.

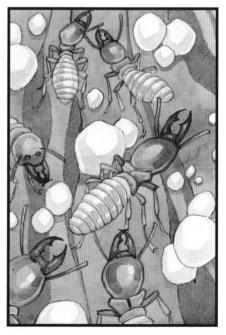

That's a lovely little home!

Thanks! I call it my dungalow.

How It Works

The double-banded courser lays its eggs near antelope poop. It's about the same color, and ideal camouflage for protecting the eggs!

Don't know what smells worse, this meat or my feet!

VULTURES' STOMACHS contain juices that can kill virtually all germs—vital for birds that feed on rotting meat. Their poop contains the same juices, so to protect themselves from germs while feeding on a carcass, they poop on their own feet!

Can We Use Poop as a Fertilizer?

It'll help the crops grow.

Yes we can! Poop is fantastic at helping plants grow. In fact, farmers have been using animal dung to fertilize their crops for at least 8,000 years! Manure, as animal dung fertilizer is called, makes soil more fertile by adding nutrients such as nitrogen, phosphorus, and potassium. It also makes the soil better at absorbing and storing water. In addition to using manure from cattle, pigs, sheep, and chickens, farmers also use guano, or bird poop. They even use specially treated human poop as manure.

It'll keep you from getting dirty.

MANURE SPREADING. Originally, manure had to be spread around the field manually. In the 1890s, Joseph Oppenheim saved farmers from this time-consuming, smelly job by inventing the widespread manure spreader.

PANDA POOP TEA. In 2012, Chinese businessman An Yanshi began selling the world's most expensive tea (priced $54,000 per pound). The secret of its unique flavor? His plants are fertilized with panda poop.

I can't go in front of you.

And then we're supposed to eat them?

You Can Do It!

To fertilize your garden, mix some manure with compost (decomposed plant matter) and spread it on your plants.

HUMANURE. Humans have been using their own poop for manure for thousands of years. Today, we first remove the harmful bacteria at a sewage plant. The remaining sludge (known as biosolids) is safe to use as a fertilizer.

GUANO MINING. Seabirds have been doing their business on the islands off Peru for thousands of years, leaving guano deposits up to 150 feet (46 m) deep! People mine it because it makes an excellent fertilizer for their crops.

Crazy humans!

Can Poop Give Us Power?

It may seem strange to think that the stuff we flush down our toilets could help light our homes—but it's true! Poop power has been used for thousands of years. The ancient Egyptians lit their cooking fires with dry animal dung, and the Assyrians burned biogas (gaseous fuel) made from human waste to heat their bathwater. It's a cheap, plentiful form of fuel, though it does cause a lot of pollution. Today, we can create much cleaner, greener fuels from poop. With anaerobic digestion, feces is converted into biogas, which can provide heat and electricity. And biogas can be converted into an eco-friendly vehicle fuel called biomethane.

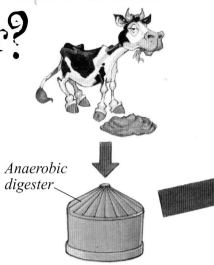

Anaerobic digester

ANAEROBIC DIGESTION
1. The poop is placed in a sealed vessel (an anaerobic digester) with no oxygen. The vessel is then warmed.

It's all about recycling!

2. Bacteria turns the poop into biogas, which can be burned to generate heat and power.

Biogas

3. Carbon dioxide can be removed from biogas to form biomethane, which can be used as gas power or as a transport fuel.

Fuel tower

How It Works

In rural India they use cow dung, rice straw, and water to make "pies" that are used for cooking fuel.

It takes five years' worth of one person's poop to fill its tank.

The solar panels will catch the Sun here.

THE POOP BUS. The "Bio-Bus," which operates in Bristol, England, is powered by a combination of human feces and household waste, converted into biomethane.

HYDRO-TOILET. A research team has built a toilet that uses solar power to extract hydrogen from human waste. The remaining waste can be used as fertilizer, while the hydrogen is siphoned off for later use as energy.

Yes, but it's not very private.

Can Poop Make Us Healthy?

We've already looked at how poop can make us sick, so it might seem odd to be told that poop can also make us healthy—but it can! For one thing, poop can help diagnose illness. By examining a sample of your stool, doctors can identify diseases in your digestive system and see how well your liver and pancreas are working. Poop can also make us better! With a stool transplant, doctors take poop from a healthy person and transplant it into someone suffering from an intestinal disease. The bacteria in the healthy poop replaces the sick person's gut bacteria and helps them fight the disease.

WHY "STOOL"? Poop is sometimes called "stool" because a "stool of ease" or "close stool" was something people sat on when using a chamber pot in Tudor times.

You said you wanted to see my stool.

NO BACTERIA. Koalas are born without bacteria in their intestines. They must eat their mother's poop to get the bacteria they need to digest their food.

How It Works

Bolivian silver mines pollute local rivers. The rivers can be cleaned with llama dung, as bacteria in the dung absorb harmful acids.

NIGHTINGALES in Japan are reared on a diet of seeds and berries. People then use their guano as a facial—it supposedly tightens and refreshes the skin!

CAMEL POOP. During World War II, German soldiers in North Africa discovered a cure for dysentery from the locals: eating fresh camel dung!

POOP SHIELD. Astronauts heading to Mars will be exposed to dangerous cosmic rays. The solution? Line the spacecraft's walls with their own poop!

What Other Ways Do We Use Poop?

Poop is useful to us in lots of ways—for example, in animal tracking and conservation. Experts can identify animals from their poop (or scat). Dogs, bears, and raccoons leave thick, tube-shaped scat. Big cat scat is teardrop-shaped, while rabbit and deer scat is small and round. From a single piece of elephant dung, an expert can figure out the animal's age, size, gender, diet, and health, and also when it was last in that area.

I'd say this one was big, angry, and... not far away.

How It Works

Tanners once used dog poop when tanning leather. They kneaded the skins with a mixture of poop and water. Bacteria in the poop helped to soften the leather.

WHALE POOP can tell us a lot about the animals, including their stress levels. Scientists noticed a drop in whale stress after the 9/11 terrorist attacks, when shipping was halted.

COW-CHIP THROWING is a popular sport in the rural midwestern United States. A cow chip is a dry, disc-shaped piece of cow dung.

CAMEL-FLAGE. In North Africa during World War II, the Allies planted land mines that looked like camel dung.

INSECTS adore fresh cow dung, but they hate the smoke when dry dung is burned. In Africa, people burn cow dung as a way to repel mosquitoes that carry malaria.

POOP ART. In 2013, a San Francisco gallery hosted an art show of paintings made from animal feces.

What Can We Make From Poop?

Poop can be made into many useful things. For example, cow dung has traditionally been used as a building material. It can be used as cement or to line walls and flooring for insulation. The dung dries hard like cement and emits no smell. In rural India, some outhouses are made entirely of cow dung. Once dry, they are strong enough to withstand powerful monsoon winds. In 2009, Indonesian students developed cow-dung building bricks. The bricks are 20 percent stronger and lighter than clay bricks, and avoid the environmental damage that can be caused by quarrying.

POOP PAPER. In Thailand, to raise money for elephant conservation projects, people are making fine stationery paper from elephant dung. Here's how they do it:
1. Wash and boil the dung for five hours.
2. Spin for three hours to cut the fibers.
3. Divide into equal balls.
4. Sift into frames.
5. Dry in the Sun.
6. Sand to a smooth surface.

1.

2.

3.

How It Works

The Asian palm civet loves eating the fruit from coffee trees, but it only partly digests them. The beans inside the fruit that get passed in its poop are sold as a luxury coffee.

She helped me build it!

They're fighting for guano...

...to make gunpowder...

...so they can keep fighting.

4.

5.

6.

GUNPOWDER GUANO. Guano is full of potassium nitrate, which is used to make gunpowder. The War of the Pacific (1879–1883) between Chile, Peru, and Bolivia was partly fought for the right to mine guano.

What Can We Learn From Ancient Poop?

For most of human history, we managed without toilets and sewers and pooped pretty much wherever we pleased. This means there's plenty of ancient poop out there— or paleofeces, to give it its technical name. We can learn about how people used to live by studying paleofeces. The diet and health of ancient peoples is revealed by analyzing the seeds, small bones, and parasite eggs in their poop. Archaeologists can even extract the DNA of the person who produced the poop, as well as the DNA of what he or she ate.

I hope you're not becoming a vegetarian.

THE OLDEST POOP. Archaeologists used to believe Neanderthals ate only meat, but the discovery of some 50,000-year-old poop has revealed that they also dined on berries, nuts, and vegetables.

CRUSADERS had parasites in their poop. Researchers studying feces from a 12th-century castle in Cyprus found eggs of the giant roundworm, which can grow up to a foot (30.5 centimeters) long and lives in the intestines, stealing nutrients from its host.

We'll starve in this siege.

I'm already starving.

Archaeologists can study paleofeces to learn about changes in the diet of ancient peoples, and even (by analyzing digested pollen) what time of year a site was occupied. This can teach us such things as when people first started farming.

FOSSIL FECES of two ancient South American peoples proved they had different diets, despite living close together. The Saladoids' poop showed a preference for fish, while the Huecoids' feces revealed a liking for maize (corn) and fungi.

KILLED BY POOP. Vast numbers of animals were wiped out by a 50-year drought 4,200 years ago on Mauritius. Studies of the sediment showed that their excrement got mixed into their water supply, killing them.

Does Poop Affect the Environment?

Poop can be very bad for the environment. Dog poop can damage lawns and contaminate waterways with harmful bacteria. Cow dung pollutes the atmosphere with methane and nitrous oxide, adding to global warming. Run-off from cow dung increases nitrogen and phosphorus levels in waterways, causing blooms of algae that can kill fish and aquatic plants. But poop can also do a lot of good. Whale poop, for example, releases nitrogen and iron into the ocean, helping the growth of organisms that fish depend on.

SEA CUCUMBERS help to build coral reefs by digesting sand and excreting calcium carbonate, a mineral needed in coral formation.

There are 1.5 billion cows on this planet, each producing 150 pounds of dung a day. That's a lot of pollution!

We're lying on fish poop!

Top Tip

Flush dog waste down the toilet or wrap it in a doggie bag and throw it in the trash.

BUILDING ISLANDS. When the parrot fish feeds on seaweed, it catches bits of coral in its beak, which it poops out as sand. Over time, parrot fish have played a part in building some Caribbean islands in this way.

FAKE POOP. Mollusks eat everything! What they can't digest, they wrap in mucus and excrete separately. This "fake poop" helps clean the oceans of pollutants like farm waste.

I'll have everything, please.

I'm doing my part for the environment!

PANDA POOP contains a bacterium that can break down extremely tough plant material, which could help in the development of biofuels.

WORM CASTING is the polite term for worm poop. Castings fertilize the soil by adding nutrients and helpful bacteria.

What Happens to Poop?

So you've gone to the bathroom. You've flushed. What happens next to your poop? Well, the poop (now known as sewage) joins urine and household wastewater in a long series of pipes, which eventually lead to a sewage treatment plant. Even though poop is messy, smelly, and sometimes dangerous, you now know that it has many important uses that you wouldn't want to live without!

Sewage arrives at treatment plant.

SEWAGE TREATMENT PLANTS are places where sewage is converted into products that are safe to be released back into the environment. The sewage passes through a series of filters, which clean it of impurities. Once cleaned, solid waste (sludge) is either dried and sold to farmers as fertilizer or dumped in landfill or at sea. Purified liquid waste is released into rivers and streams.

Sewage passes through a filter called a **grit tank** *where large pieces of waste, including household trash and pieces of grit, are removed.*

FECES IN THE OCEANS. Ships are allowed to dump untreated sewage overboard as long as they are more than 12 miles (19 kilometers) from land. This pollution endangers marine life.

PLANE POOP. Between 1979 and 2001, at least 27 balls of frozen poop fell from planes in the U.S. alone. Today, airplanes use vacuum toilets, which suck the waste into a sealed holding tank for the duration of the flight.

WASTE IN SPACE. There are close to 100 bags of poop on the moon, left there over the years by astronauts of Apollo missions. The lack of wind and rain mean they're still perfectly preserved.

Hōw It Works

A new invention being created called the Ashpoopie will scoop up dog poop and vaporize it in less than a minute, turning it into germfree, odorless ash.

*The remaining sewage is pumped into a **sedimentation tank** where bacteria consume organic matter and produce methane.*

*Liquid waste may be passed through an **activated sludge tank** where bacteria feed on organic matter.*

Clean water out

Sprinkler

*In some plants, liquid waste is passed through a **trickling filter** system, where it is sprayed onto a bed of rocks covered in a slime layer of bacteria that purifies it.*

Solid waste sinks to the bottom of the tank to form sludge.

Sludge out

Clean water out

Glossary

Algae A family of simple, non-flowering organisms.

Anaerobic digestion A process by which bacteria break down organic matter in the absence of oxygen.

Bacteria Single-celled micro-organisms, some of which can cause disease.

Biofuel A fuel obtained from living matter.

Biogas A gaseous fuel (e.g., methane), produced by the breakdown of organic matter in the absence of oxygen.

Biomethane A purified form of biogas that can be used as natural gas.

Compost Decayed organic matter that can be used as a plant fertilizer.

Cosmic rays Highly energetic particles that travel through space at speeds approaching the speed of light.

Defecate Excrete poop.

DNA A type of molecule found in all living things. It carries genetic information (the information that determines an organism's characteristics).

Dysentery A disease of the intestines that causes severe diarrhea.

Eco-friendly Not harmful to the environment.

Excrete Expel waste.

Feces Waste matter discharged from the intestines after food has been digested. Another word for poop.

Fiber A substance found in foods such as cereals, which resists digestion and helps move digested food through the intestines.

Global warming A gradual increase in the temperature of Earth's atmosphere caused by increased levels of carbon dioxide and other pollutants.

Gut bacteria The community of microorganisms that live in the intestines of animals.

Intestine The lower part of the digestive system, from the end of the stomach to the anus.

Larva The immature form of an insect.

Liver A large organ that helps turn the products of digestion into substances useful to the body.

Malaria A disease caused by a parasite that invades the red blood cells.

Manure Animal dung used as fertilizer.

Mollusk A family of animals that live in damp or watery habitats. They include snails, clams, and mussels.

Monsoon A wind in South and Southeast Asia that blows May to September, bringing rain (wet monsoon), and then again from October to April (dry monsoon).

Neanderthal An extinct species of human that lived in Europe 120,000–35,000 years ago.

Nutrient A substance that provides nourishment needed for growth and healthy life.

Pancreas A large organ located behind the stomach that plays an important part in the digestive process.

Parasite An organism that lives in or on another organism (its host) and takes nutrients from the host.

Sanitation Facilities needed for public health, such as a supply of clean drinking water and adequate forms of sewage disposal.

Sewage Solid and liquid waste carried in sewers.

Virus A tiny organism that can reproduce and grow only when inside living cells. Viruses cause diseases such as influenza (flu), the common cold, and gastroenteritis (stomach flu).

Index

Top Weirdest Uses for Animal Poop

Poop-powered light: In a park in Massachusetts, dog owners dump their pets' mess into "digesters" that convert the methane in the poop into gas fuel, which then powers the park's street lamp at night.

The Loowatt was created by designer Virginia Gardiner to help bring sanitation and energy to developing countries. It is a waterless toilet made of molded horse dung. When it's full, the waste can be dumped in a digester and turned into fuel.

Chicken feed: The larvae of the black soldier fly live on and in feces. They can turn manure into compost within a week and are also rich in protein. Scientists are now testing their potential as food for chickens.

Pothole filler: Elephant poop is often used to fill up holes in the roads in South Africa's Kapama Game Reserve.

Health treatments: In traditional Chinese medicine, flying squirrel poop is applied to the skin to help improve blood circulation, and silkworm poop is used to treat stress.

The Poop Bus

The "Bio-Bus," as it is officially known, began running between the English cities of Bristol and Bath in November 2014. Each day it fills up its tank at a site in Avonmouth, Bristol, where human sewage and inedible food waste from 32,000 households is converted into biomethane gas, the bus's fuel. The poop-powered bus, which can seat up to 40 people, can travel up to 186 miles (300 km) on one tank of gas. A single person's annual food and sewage waste would fuel the Bio-Bus for 37 miles (60 km). Up to 10,000 passengers use the bus each month, and many of them no doubt help to fuel it.

How Does It Work?

The biomethane gas is made by anaerobic digestion. The human and food waste is poured into oxygen-free digesters where bacteria get to work breaking it down to produce methane-rich biogas. The biogas is upgraded to biomethane gas, suitable for transport fuel, by removing the carbon dioxide and adding propane. The compressed gas is stored in dome-like tanks on the roof of the Bio-Bus. The bus's engine works similarly to a diesel engine in a regular bus.

Why Do It?

The makers of the Bio-Bus believe that it offers a clean and sustainable alternative to conventional buses. It produces 30 percent less carbon dioxide than diesel engines, and its exhaust is virtually odor-free. The fuel is also infinitely renewable!